Copyright © April 2024 Nikki Walker
All rights reserved. This document is geared towards providing exact and reliable information with regard to the topic and issue covered. The publication is sold with the idea that the publisher is not required to render accounting, officially permitted, or otherwise, qualified services. If advice is necessary, legal or professional, a practiced individual in the profession should be ordered.

No part of this publication may be reproduced, duplicated, distributed, or transmitted in any form or by any means, including photocopying, recording, or other electronic or mechanical methods, without the prior written permission of the publisher, except in the case of brief quotations embodied in critical reviews and certain other noncommercial uses permitted by copyright law. Recording of this publication is strictly prohibited and any storage of this document is not allowed unless with written permission from the publisher. All rights reserved.

The information provided herein is stated to be truthful and consistent, in that any liability, in terms of inattention or otherwise, by any usage or abuse of any policies, processes, or directions contained within is the solitary and utter responsibility of the recipient reader. Under no circumstances will any legal responsibility or blame be held against the publisher for any reparation, damages, or monetary loss due to the information herein, either directly or indirectly.

Respective authors own all copyrights not held by the publisher.
Printed by Kiyanni B., Write It Out Publishing, LLC. in the United States of America.
Write It Out Publishing LLC
Virginia Beach, Virginia
Writeitoutpublishing.com

ISBN: 979-8-9893223-2-9
Book Cover Illustrator: Maurice Rogers
Editors: Renee Johnson and Tamira K. Butler-Likely

First printing, (e-book or paperback) 4/24/2024
Author: Dr. Nikki Walker (Ki-Juana Walker)
PO Box 2371 Chesapeake, VA 23327
Author Email: nikkisellsva@gmail.com

MILLENNIAL LEADERSHIP DEVELOPMENT:

FOR TODAY'S ORGANIZATIONS

VIRGINIA BEACH, VA

FOR TODAY'S ORGANIZATIONS

MILLENNIAL LEADERSHIP DEVELOPMENT

NIKKI WALKER

13.
CHAPTER 1:
OVERVIEW OF THE FUTURE OF WORK

21.
CHAPTER 2:
STRATEGIC FORESIGHT AND CHANGE

35.
CHAPTER 3:
GENERATION X VS. MILLENNIALS

45.
CHAPTER 4:
LEADERSHIP STYLES

65.
CHAPTER 5:
LEADERSHIP COMPETENCIES

73.
CHAPTER 6:
COACHING FOR MILLENNIAL LEADERSHIP DEVELOPMENT

79.
CONCLUSION

INTRODUCTION

The task of developing Millennial leaders is imperative for today's organizations. Organizations must first know where they are going to have a great future. In an era of constant innovation, it is critical to understand that the future of work in any organization will involve Millennials (those born between 1984 and 2002). After all, this generation will represent nearly 75 percent of the workforce by 2025. Operating your organization from the past will cause you to presently encounter leadership development challenges and demands that require solutions. The pathway to growing a successful organization is to grow Millennial leaders. Without a coaching plan in place to develop Millennials as great leaders, even the most brilliant and innovative organizations will not maximize their potential for success.

Millennial Island – An Illustration

Are you and your organization ready for Millennial leaders and their launch into leadership? Your organization must stay agile, because Millennials are a significant part of your future workforce. To set the stage for our leadership experience, let's take some time to think about leadership with a fun illustration. Take out a sheet of paper and imagine that you and your team are stranded on Millennial Island. There are no other people or buildings on the island; however, you and your team have to survive until you are rescued. One of the Millennials on your team found a motorboat that is big enough to carry your team, but it has no fuel. Although the Millennial found the boat, he does not know how to drive it. To fuel up and drive the boat, you can only use leadership qualities that Millennials should value. What leadership qualities would be great ones to power the boat? Some examples are patience, leading by example, honesty, communication, confidence, positivity, commitment, creativity, and empathy. On your paper, begin to write down qualities that would help the Millennial leader soar in their leadership capacity and potential.

Illustration Takeaways

What leadership qualities did you select to power your

organizational boat to get it moving to your city? Before we deep dive into this book, it is important to know that the effectiveness of your organization is directly dependent on the effectiveness of your leaders. Millennials want to be leaders! Now, let's begin with learning how you can create meaningful leadership development experiences to prepare Millennials for future leadership roles.

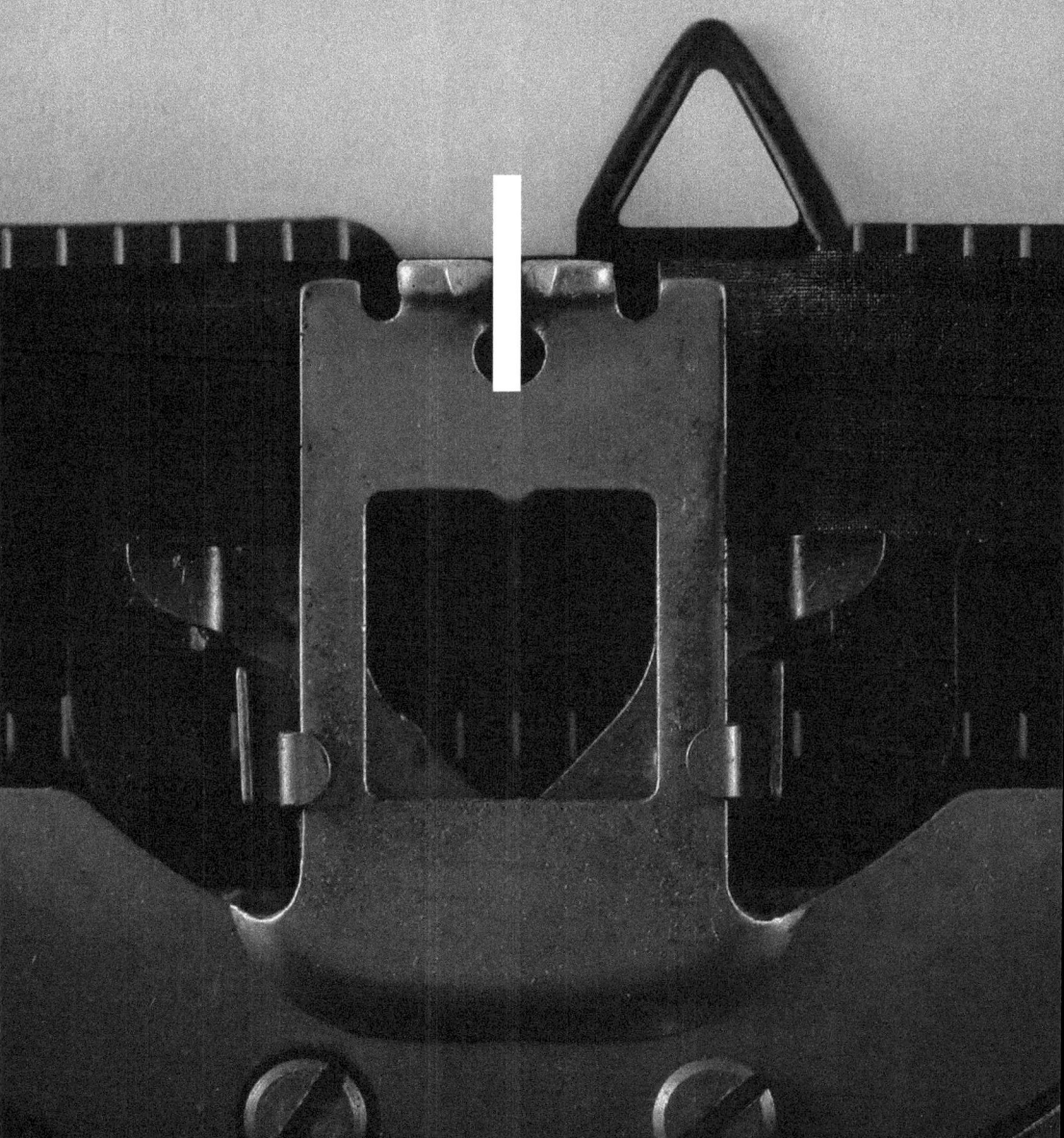

CHAPTER 1:

OVERVIEW OF THE FUTURE OF WORK

To start, understanding the future of work is important! Organizations are powerful incubators for the development of leaders. The future of work is occurring right now. Leaders must adapt their skills to the changing needs of the workplace to move toward the organization's goals, while creating a motivating environment for people to realize those goals. However, organizations must cultivate an environment where leaders *want* to be there versus *needing* to be there.

Many organizations around the world today are in trouble. The world of work is changing around them while they remain stagnant. The larger the gap grows, the greater the chance that these organizations will not survive. However, organizations should not merely want to survive, but rather they must also seek to thrive and be competitive in a new, rapidly changing world.[1] The future of work brings new attitudes and ways of work to which leaders must adapt. Questions that need to be answered as it pertains to the future of work are:[2]

- What trends are driving the future of work?
- How will these changes impact the way employees work, the way managers lead, and how organizations are structured?
- What needs to be done to adapt to these changes?

Things change so quickly, which means that we must start to strategically plan now to achieve a future that we would like to see in organizations down the road.

SEVEN PREDICTIONS FOR THE FUTURE OF WORK

I want to share with you seven predictions for the future of work that will affect what is ahead for your organization. These seven predictions are significant because organizations must prepare and take concrete steps that support continuous transformation in a rapidly changing world.

AUTOMATION

---

[1] Morgan, J. (2014). The future of work: Attract new talent, build better leaders, and create a competitive organization. San Francisco, CA: Wiley.
[2] Ibid.

The "good ole days" of 9 to 5 will soon be history. As we are already beginning to experience, robotic process automation will continue to replace people in completing repetitive, time-consuming work, such as client profile updates, insurance claims processing, credit card applications, and healthcare patient registrations. Virtual robot assistants will assume former human duties such as auto-correspondence, appointment scheduling, and other functions.[3] Automation is important

because the human-to-machine collaboration technologies will make organizations more intelligent and greatly improve overall human work performance to drive business value. By 2025, 25 percent of working professionals will use digital assistants and 58 percent of organizations will invest in virtual assistant technology. Have you considered how virtual assistants can change your organizational dynamics?

BANKING

The future for banking means that personal financial advisors will

[3]Ardi, D. "7 Predictions for the Future of Work." February 13, 2014. Retrieved from https://www.fastcompany.com/3026345/7-predictions-for-the-future-of-work

be accessible at all times via tablets, phones, and Google Home or Echo technology. These personal financial advisors will manage your finances, enabling people to avoid visiting a physical bank. These advisors will balance your accounts, check your credit, and give advice about paying debts.[4] Social media technology will also transform the way the world operates with banks. Relationship managers will connect with banking clients via preferred networks such as Facebook Messenger, Google Hangouts, and WhatsApp.[5]

HEALTHCARE

In the healthcare sector, patients will generate their own data on their smartphones. Healthcare data analytics will help doctors produce immediate answers for care. Mobile care services will provide care to patients at home, work, or at school via tablets and smartphones.[6] Likewise, patients will be equipped with remote monitoring where sensors will record vital signs and transmit them to doctors. Those sensors will provide warning signals to doctors to trigger a physician phone call or visit. The future of healthcare will also welcome robots that will perform surgeries and administer vaccinations, replacing traditional physicians and nurses.[7]

AVATARS

Avatars are predicted to function as virtual figures posing as ideal clients to help businesses determine the best target audiences for products and services. Avatars also will be used in virtual reality and act on behalf of people and organizations to conduct high-level tasks, such as performing extensive research, posting blogs and social media updates, and managing the daily activities of businesses. Can you imagine avatars designing products and running virtual stores in the future?

---

[4]Meola, A. (2016). "The Future of banking: Growth of Innovation Banking Fintech Services." Retrieved from http://www.businessinsider.com/the-future-of-banking-growth-of-innovative-banking-fintech-services-2016-12
[5]Lurinavicius, T. (2017). "What is the future of digital banking?" Retrieved from https://thenextweb.com/contributors/2017/08/27/future-of-digital-banking/
[6]Topol, E. (2016). The patient will see you now: The future of medicine is in your hands. New York, NY: Basic Books.
[7]Acton, A. (2017). "What You Need to Know About the Future of Healthcare." Retrieved from https://www.forbes.com/sites/annabelacton/2017/07/14/the-future-of-health-its-in-your-hands/#31d2f4e62af2

THE HUMAN CLOUD

The Human Cloud is a natural evolution of outsourcing activities offshore but is much more significant and powerful. The Human Cloud will reshape established business practices, reshape organizational structures, and profoundly change economic labor models. The Human Cloud incorporates outsourcing, crowdsourcing, micro-sourcing, and marketplaces into an integrated and seamless connection between people and technology.[8] Employees are starting to see the Human Cloud as a new way to get work done. White-collar jobs are chopped into hundreds of distinct projects or tasks, then scattered into a virtual "cloud" of willing workers who could be anywhere in the world, as long as they have an internet connection.[9]

THE FUTURE OF ORGANIZATIONS – WORK IN ACTION

In an age where skill sets can become obsolete in just a few years, many workers and organizations are struggling to stay current. Since organizations are powerful incubators for the development of leaders, organizations should encourage continuous learning, improve individual mobility, and foster a growth mindset in every employee, year after year. Three driving forces will have a significant effect on work and the workplace, the new realities of work:[10]

- Technology: Technology continues to drive the nature of work and demanding organizations to redesign most jobs. Over time, artificial intelligence, automation, robotics, and algorithms are replacing human job talent. New skills will leverage empathy, social and emotional intelligence, and the ability to set context and define business problems.

- Skill Sets: Likewise, employees will need to learn new skills

---

[8]April, L. (2016). "The Human Cloud in 2017: Tech Trends That Will Define the Next Year." Retrieved from http://www.crowdstaffing.com/blog/human-cloud-2017-tech-trends

[9]Ibid.

[10]Hagel, J., Schwartz, J., & Bersin, J. (2017). Navigating the future of work: Can we point business, workers, and social institutions in the same direction. Retrieved from https://www2.deloitte.com/dup-us-en/deloitte-review/issue-21/navigating-new-forms-of-work.html

to remain employable. Such skills for workers of the future would be cultivating creativity, collaboration, abstract and systems design thinking, communication, and the aptitude to thrive in different environments.

- Coronavirus Pandemic: The recent coronavirus pandemic has made a lasting impact on the future of work. Organizations will need to rethink workforce and employee planning, management, and performance strategies. Gone will be full-time, benefits, and defined salaries. In turn, workers will have alternative work arrangements such as remote working, freelancing, crowdsourcing, and contract-based work.

WHAT WILL ORGANIZATIONS NEED TO OPERATE IN THE FUTURE?

Organizations that invest in employees are more productive, valuable, attractive, innovative, and profitable, and have superior performance over those who don't. There is tremendous value in building amazing teams and transforming how work is done to positively impact business results.

Future organizations will need:[11]

- A global mindset with smaller teams – employees will need to frame-shift to address various business conditions in different locations for the generation of balanced and innovative solutions.

- A connected, multigenerational workforce – a diverse and united team will enable organizations to build new strategies and ways of working to create adaptable and culturally agile organizations.

- Leaders who are intrapreneurial – this term speaks to

---

[11] Morgan, J. (2017). The employee experience advantage: How to win the war for talent by giving employees the workspaces they want, the tools they need, and a culture they can celebrate. San Francisco, CA: Wiley.

entrepreneurial thinking within organizations. Intrapreneurial leaders are creative risk-takers who unearth entrepreneurial culture, achieve growth agendas, and innovate inside their organizations.

- Technological savvy and cloud-based functions – investments in technology take collaboration and communication to greater levels in business environments.

- More women in senior management roles – organizations will need to diversify their work structures by moving women into leadership roles to address gender equity.

- A flatter organizational structure – a less top-to-bottom approach within leadership breaks up the traditional hierarchical structure of one-way communication and power at the top. A flatter structure opens up lines of communication and collaboration and leverages all levels in the organization for increased involvement in decision-making.

- The ability to leverage storytelling to build relationships within and outside the organization to energize and inspire teams to be more collaborative and authentic.

As organizations become increasingly fast paced, and as constant change becomes the new normal, stories can play a pivotal role in keeping Millennials engaged, educated, and inspired. The usage of storytelling enables leaders to inspire Millennials by creating images and representations to communicate leadership principles. From there, Millennial leaders can grow to function as transformational storytellers that understand the structure and logic of their industries, while developing people and business strategies that translate into powerful and accomplished organizational plans and goals.

STORYTELLING IN ACTION

Storytelling reinforces collaboration, encouraging people to work together via narratives to illustrate organizational goals. At Southwest Airlines, CEO Robert Jordan uses storytelling as a means to share triumphant stories. When addressing the company's 74,800 employees about providing exceptional service to customers, Kelly uses stories and costumes that illustrate examples of Southwest employees who excel at service. In addition, he uses videos for storytelling that celebrate real "in the trenches" stories, to help employees visualize what the corporate culture and purpose of Southwest Airlines look and feel like.

At FedEx, stories circulate about drivers who go the extra mile in delivering packages to customers. These stories not only help employees to "see and hear" the mission and values of FedEx, but they show the promise of reliability and extraordinary work. When organizations seize the power of stories, the weight of each story becomes a great teacher of strategy and organizational learning that benefits the organization.

Let's dive deeper into leveraging strategic foresight and change to examine Millennial leadership development further.

1. What does the future of your organization look like?

2. If you could retrace your steps, what are some ways in which you could have strategically planned to achieve the future you would like to see currently in your organization?

3. Share a few instances where your storytelling has helped people and strategies transform into powerful and accomplished goals and plans.

v^2 $tg\vartheta_B = \frac{n_2}{n_1} = n_{21}$ $PV = nRT$ $\psi = \iint \vec{D} d\vec{S}$

$M_e = \sigma T^4$ $\phi_e = \frac{L}{\Delta t}$ $\int$ $\frac{\Delta\psi}{2\pi} = \frac{\Delta x}{\lambda_1} = \frac{x_2 - x_1}{x} S_2$ $V = C_r$

$\psi = E\psi$ $\Delta t' = \frac{\Delta t'}{\sqrt{1-\frac{v^2}{c^2}}}$ $4\pi r^2$ $k = \frac{1}{4\pi\varepsilon_0\varepsilon_r}$ $v_k = \sqrt{R\frac{M_Z}{R_Z}}$ $\vec{F}_m = B I \vec{l}$

$E = \hbar\omega$ $X_L = \frac{U_m}{I_m} = \omega L = 2\pi f L$ $F_g = $

$E = k\frac{q_1 q_2}{r^2}$ $U = W_{AB}$ $|E_{pA} - E_{pB}|$

$V = \frac{nh}{2\pi r m_e}$ $\phi_E = \frac{F_e}{q_0} = k\frac{Q}{r^2}$ $= |\psi_A - \psi_B|$ $T = \frac{4n_1 n_2}{(n_2+n_1)^2}$ $R_m = \frac{C}{T}$ $k = $

$\frac{M_m}{N_A} = \frac{M_r \cdot 10^{-3}}{N_A}$ $l_t = l_0(1+\alpha\Delta t)$ $I = \frac{U_e}{R+R_i}$ $m = N \cdot m_0$ $\frac{M_m}{N_A}$ $E = \frac{E_c}{a}\int^{+a/2}\sin(\omega t+\phi)dy$ $-a/2\,y = -\frac{tg\tau'}{tg\tau}\frac{d}{f}\omega = $

$\sqrt{m_e}$ $R = \rho\frac{l}{S}$ $E = mc^2$ $\frac{\sin\alpha}{\sin\beta} = \frac{v_1}{v_2} = \frac{n_2}{n_1}$ $V = $

$\psi(x) = \sqrt{2/L}\sin\frac{n\pi x}{L}$ $E = \frac{1}{2}\sqrt{k/m}$ $\Delta I_c \phi_e = \frac{\Delta E}{\Delta t}$ $\frac{w_1}{x} + $ $F_x = \frac{1}{2}C_x f$

$\iint \vec{J} d\vec{S}$ $\vec{S} = \frac{1}{\mu_0}(\vec{E}\times\vec{B})$ $\frac{\Delta I_B}{\phi} = \frac{2\pi\sin\vartheta}{\lambda}y$

$E_k = \frac{h^2}{8mL^2}n^2$

$\frac{N_A = \sqrt{\frac{3R_mT}{M_R \cdot 10^{-3}}}}{M_m}$ $E = \frac{\hbar^2 k^2}{2m}$ $pc = \frac{1AU}{r}$ $\oiint \vec{D} d\vec{a}$

$h = Shpg$ $f_0 = \frac{1}{2\pi\sqrt{CL}}$ $M_\odot = \frac{4\pi^2 r^3}{dt T^2}$ $\sigma = \frac{Q}{S}$ $\sum I_m^2 = U_m^2[\frac{1}{R^2}+(\frac{1}{x_c}-\frac{1}{x_L})]$ $R = \frac{U}{I}$ F_v

$\cos\frac{\vartheta_2}{2}$ $M = Fd\cos$

$(\vartheta_1 - \vartheta_2)\sin(\vartheta_1+\vartheta_2)$ $\int \vec{E}d\vec{l} = -\iint \frac{\partial\vec{B}}{\partial t}\cdot d\vec{S}$ $P = \frac{E}{C} = \frac{hf}{c} = \frac{h}{\lambda}$

$R = R_0\sqrt[3]{A}$ $\mu = U_m\sin\omega(t-\tau) = U_m$ $Q = mc\Delta t$

$\oint \vec{H}d\vec{l} = \iint(\vec{J}+\frac{\partial\vec{D}}{\partial t})\cdot d\vec{S}$ $L = 10\log\frac{I}{I_0}$ $\Delta\psi = \frac{2\pi\Delta x}{\lambda} = \frac{2\pi d\sin}{\lambda}$

$B = \mu_0\sum I_i$ $P = \frac{E}{\Delta S}$ $= \frac{m\Delta V}{\Delta S\Delta t}$ $P = UI$ $h = \frac{1}{2}gt^2$ $V - V_1$

$f' = \frac{n_a \cdot n_b}{(n-1)(n_a-n_b)}$ $\nabla\times(-\frac{\partial\vec{B}}{\partial t}) = -\frac{\partial}{\partial t}(rot\vec{B}) = -\mu_0\frac{\partial}{\partial t}$

CHAPTER 2:

STRATEGIC FORESIGHT AND CHANGE

"Insanity is continuing to do the same thing over and over and expecting different results."
- Albert Einstein

The BIG question is: How will your church or organization look in the future? How will your leadership team look? Will Millennials in your organization be successfully groomed for the future? The future of work centers on the importance of the Millennial generation. We will need Millennials in the future. They are the largest segment of the US workforce and will dominate the landscape for decades to come. It is imperative to consider how Gen X'ers and Millennials will work together to take church and business organizations into the future. Here are some questions to reflect on your organization's level of strategic foresight:

- How often does your leadership team engage in strategic conversations that include thinking about the future?

- What strategies does your leadership team use to "test out" ideas and concepts?

- How is focus kept on long-term objectives when ministry and organizational problems and pressures continually distract you?

- What strategic thinking concepts are employed in your strategy-making processes?

- How does the leadership team consistently evaluate decisions and actions born out of strategic planning meetings?

These questions are strategic to church and secular organizations alike. If your organization is serious about stepping into its preferred future, now is the time to reflect on those questions, because your future depends on it.

DISCERNING THE TIME WE LIVE IN

To see the significance of developing Millennial leaders, leadership must envision the future. Kouzes and Posner state, "Leaders should be forward-looking and have a sense of direction. Leaders must develop this capacity to envision the future by mastering these essentials: 1) discover the theme and 2) imagine the possibilities."[12] This chapter began with an introduction to strategic foresight. One of the powerful things about strategic foresight is that getting a picture of the future allows us to reflect on the present. However, getting a picture of the future requires asking key questions. One of my favorite scripture verses is found in 1 Chronicles 12:32 (New Living Translation): "From the tribe of Issachar, there were 200 leaders of the tribe with their relatives. All these men understood the signs of the times and knew the best course for Israel to take."

By utilizing strategic foresight, we assess the internal and external environments to gain a macro-view of the world to understand "the signs of the times," assess inbound future change, employ tools to understand key drivers of change, recognize how trends can impact your ministry or organization, and prepare to engage the possible futures that can emerge.[13] From there, your organization will be equipped with strategies that encourage Millennial leadership development.

KODAK – A REAL-LIFE EXAMPLE OF THE FAILURE TO ADAPT

---

[12] Kouzes, J.M. & Posner, B.Z. (2002). The leadership challenge (3rd ed.). San Francisco, CA: Jossey-Bass.

[13] Chermack, T.J. (2011). Scenario planning in organizations: How to create, use, and assess scenarios. San Francisco, CA: Berrett-Koehler.

Do you remember Kodak? This organization (founded in the late 1880s) was a leader in the photography industry for 100-plus years, yet they failed to employ strategic foresight to remain relevant in changing technological times. Kodak was considered a global innovator in the world of photography. However, in the 1980s, the photography industry shifted to digital pictures. In Kodak's success, the company became change-resistant and lost its footing with the emergence of digital cameras. The company's first mistake was the inability to embrace the new photography business models unearthed by disruptive change.

From there, Kodak became complacent and failed to reinvent itself as the smartphone revolution disrupted the digital camera market. Because of their failure to adapt, Kodak filed for bankruptcy in 2012. Kodak's leaders did not transform their strategies and innovations because they lacked strategic creativity and foresight to see the huge opportunities to shift their business toward the digital age. Remember: Strategic foresight helps organizational leaders "think outside the box" by challenging hidden assumptions they have about the future. For Kodak, what is evident from a technological perspective is that they did not seriously consider the advent of the digital age. When the digital camera emerged, this became disruptive to Kodak's position in the industry of photography. Considering Kodak's example, what will happen if your organization does not adapt to engage, coach, and develop Millennial leaders toward the future? Let's bring it all together. In today's world, not engaging Millennials in organizations can be likened to how Kodak missed ripe opportunities to adapt and evolve. Millennials present a challenge to organizations to embrace innovation and change to work collaboratively for a sustainable future.

STRATEGIC FORESIGHT – IN DEPTH

In the twenty-first century, church and business organizations need to be more innovative to stay relevant. Strategic foresight helps organizational leaders to think strategically and ask "what if" questions that stimulate the development of strategies in light of various futures that can occur.[14] From there, scenarios can be used to "wind tunnel" and "stress test" existing strategies. This simply means that organizations will see how their strategies hold up under various scenarios. For instance, a focal question is, "How should we develop Millennial leaders?" Based on the various scenarios created, leaders will test the robustness of their decision by analyzing the strengths, weaknesses, opportunities, and threats (SWOT) embedded in each scenario.[15] Action plans are then designed and executed for implementation.

Strategic foresight helps to stimulate creativity and innovation by examining potential opportunities that can emerge in different scenarios. One example of this is found within the online retail giant, Amazon. Amazon is known for being a powerhouse online retailer. The company uses strategic foresight to stay relevant among its competitors by seeing what is ahead and seizing opportunities. Amazon's response to the COVID-19 pandemic has enabled the company to survive in trying times. Amazon's leadership team scanned the internal and external environments and recognized the fact that the pandemic would be a global disruptive event. Immediately, Amazon sprang into action to prepare for the surge of orders for essential items by hiring employees and expanding its delivery services. As a result, Amazon has survived turbulent times when other online retailers have been forced to shut their doors.

Is your organization ready for change in developing Millennial leaders? Everyone must be ready for change to keep a good pulse on the internal and external environment. Leaders are needed who can navigate their enterprise or ministry through the turbulence of change in order to make the organization's dream or vision a reality. The turbulence that comes with any kind of change does not necessarily mean that an organization's preferred future will be secure. Leaders are needed to move the organization forward despite the challenges that may come.

STRATEGIC THINKING

A popular statement on strategic thinking states that the only

---

[14]Motti, V.V., & Masoumi, M. (2016). An operational process for organizational foresight and anticipation. World Futures Review, 8(2), 114-125.
[15]Hines, A., & Bishop, P. (Eds). Thinking about the future: Guideline for strategic foresight. Washington, D.C. Social Technologies, LLC.

thing that remains constant is change. For organizations to survive and thrive in today's global context, leaders must anticipate and respond appropriately to change. Why are some organizations able to handle the uncertainties that abound in the external environment and thrive, while others fold under pressure? Some companies are surprised by shifts in the environment and are unable to quickly adapt to new competition, changing consumer interests, or innovative technologies.[16]

According to Hughes and Beatty, strategic thinking refers to cognitive processes required for the collection, interpretation, generation, and evaluation of information and ideas that shape an organization's sustainable competitive advantage.[17] Strategic thinking involves delving deeply into an organization's underlying assumptions and ways of thinking and acting. Strategic thinking takes into account the organization's mission and vision, and how its leaders can leverage the resources at hand to embrace and secure the organization's overarching goals and objectives.[18] A well-tested strategic framework that can engender this kind of thinking involves having engaging conversations around the organization's SWOT.[19]

SWOT

The SWOT analysis was developed for businesses and churches as a valuable tool that helps organizations step back and make an honest assessment of their present situation. It focuses on present elements of your organization to go forward futuristically. Here's an example of how the SWOT analysis would work as it relates to a church organization:

Strengths – What do we do well as a church? What is growing? Where do people seem particularly fulfilled? What community needs are we meeting? What resources are within our church community? What do we thank God for?

Weaknesses – What appears to be declining/is stagnant?

---

[16]Gordon, A. (2008). *Future savvy: Identifying trends to make better decisions, manage uncertainty, and profit for change.* New York, NY: AMACOM.

[17]Hughes, R.L. & Beatty, K.C. (2006). *Becoming a strategic leader: Your role in your organization's enduring success.* San Francisco, CA: Jossey-Bass.

[18]Cornish, E. (2004). *Futuring: The exploration of the future.* Bethesda, MD: World Future Society.

[19]Canton, J. (2015). *Future smart: Managing the game-changing trends that will transform your world.* Boston, MA: Da Capo Press.

Which areas of church seem tired or too busy? What community needs are we not meeting? Who or what needs our prayers?

Opportunities – What gifts/people/resources are under-utilized? Do we have strengths that can be built upon? Are there people/situations in the community where we could make a difference? Do we have partners in the community? How can we develop Millennial leaders?

Threats – Are any of our weaknesses becoming serious? What changes in society are affecting us? Are changes in the community affecting us? Is a lack of resources jeopardizing our future? Are we moving in fear as we launch out to build new strategies?

As seen in this exercise, the SWOT analysis is a powerful tool to identify areas for growth as an organization moves into the future with certainty and paves the path for effective strategic planning.

STRATEGIC PLANNING

From the SWOT analysis, your organization then moves into strategic planning. This incorporates taking into consideration the organization's resources and capabilities in light of its vision for the future and outlining actionable steps to achieve the preferred future state.[20] To flesh this out, what is uncovered from strategic thinking and the SWOT analysis transforms into a step-by-step methodology that takes into account your organization's mission, what you are not willing to compromise (values), and how you are going to get to the future (planning).[21] You and your organization will have the freedom to think creatively without an artificial or rigid framework that will halt innovation.

TIMES OF CRITICAL UNCERTAINTY

---

[20] Agbor, E. (2008). *Creativity and innovation: The leadership dynamics.* Journal of Strategic Leadership, 1(1), 39-45.
[21] Ibid.

Let's face it: Change creates uncertainty. Leading through change is not an easy feat. However, it must be done for organizations to survive and thrive. Leaders must recognize and respond to critical areas of uncertainty that may impact the organization's effectiveness in accomplishing its mission and vision.[22] As discussed earlier, discerning the times will help leaders to look and see what is happening on the horizon. The COVID-19 pandemic has impacted the global economy, causing social isolation, lockdowns, unemployment, and dramatic shifts in consumer behavior. In the changing global landscape, many organizations have needed to retool and pivot quickly and innovatively to survive. Disney+ has created value during the COVID-19 pandemic due to movie theater and movie studio shutdowns, and families and individuals being stuck at home during shelter-in-place orders. In the midst of its competitors, Netflix and Apple+, Disney+ made recent headlines when the company scanned the horizon and released the highly anticipated film version of *Hamilton* for streaming. In the midst of movie theaters and movie studios retooling their business models to recover after COVID-19, Disney+ has already recognized home viewings of movies will be a "new normal" distribution channel for first-run films.

DRIVING FORCES VS. RESTRAINING FORCES

There are two main forces in our environment as it relates to change within our organizations. Driving forces are those forces that influence change and keep it going. For example, new technology, changing demographics, the economy, and changes in laws are all driving forces that can impact individuals, families, and organizations.[23] In contrast, there are also restraining forces that restrain or impede the change process. Restraining forces are those forces that have the potential to hinder an organization from achieving its goals.

Let's talk about driving forces that will prove to be significant with respect to their impact on the future of Christian leadership in a

---

[22] Hodges, J. & Gill, R. (2014). *Sustaining change in organizations*. Thousand Oaks, CA: Sage Publications.

[23] Burke, W.W. & Noumair, D.A. (2015). Organization development: A process of learning and changing. Upper Saddle River, NJ: Pearson Equipment.

ministry's organizational concept.

CLERGY SHORTAGE

One driving force is the shortage of full-time pastors and ministry leaders. Chang notes how many Millennials (defined in the study as those born between 1984 and 2002) express a desire to choose a job that is meaningful and makes an impact.[24] Despite these ambitions, fewer look to ministry as a career, making it a struggle for church leaders to appoint and equip younger successors. More than two-thirds of today's pastors (69 percent) say it has become harder to identify suitable pastor candidates among Millennials.[25] Pastors of small congregations, with a smaller pool of potential leaders, were more likely to agree.

This trend can significantly impact ministry organizations with respect to the recruitment, retention, and deployment of these leaders to fill future leadership roles and gaps. So, what are the implications of this trend as it relates to leadership? If these trends continue as they are with respect to the widening age difference of those who are currently serving in ministry, it is apparent that churches and other ministries will have a leadership gap crisis on their hands. Also, this trend will necessitate leadership development initiatives be put in place where younger ministry leaders are groomed to come into leadership positions when older leaders retire.

In other words, the leadership pipeline should account for leadership transitions and diversity in the ministry's structure. Ministry organizations that do not have a leadership pipeline in place will have challenges with the strength and depth of their leadership bench, both in the present and future.

AGING POPULATION

The aging population is another significant driver of change, which is impacting ministry organizations in the present and will continue into the future. Approximately two billion people will become sixty years

---

[24]Patricia Chang, "A Quick Question: Is There a Clergy Shortage?," Hartford Institute for Religion Research, October 2, 2013, accessed December 2, 2017, http://hirr.hartsem.edu/research/quick_question28.html.
[25]Ibid.

of age and older by 2050.[26] Statistics also confirm the population of the US is also aging. Some projections state the number of older people will increase by 135 percent between 2000 and 2050.[27] Younger age participation in churches is decreasing rather than increasing. This presents tangible challenges in terms of sustaining the organization through finances, the vibrancy that can exist where there are intergenerational relationships, as well as imparting the Gospel of the Kingdom to the next generation.

Again, what are the implications of this trend as it relates to leadership? Organizations will need to find ways to stimulate intergenerational collaboration between aging members, younger members, and ministry leaders. This speaks to organizational culture. Organizational culture is defined as the mutually reinforcing "web" of those beliefs and practices as they are held, tested, and evolved over time in an organization.[28] If your leaders desire to respond strategically to continued aging of members in their congregation, as well as engage the younger generation, then organizational culture cannot be ignored. Seasoned leaders are needed to bridge the generational gap and collaborate to ensure that the organizational vision and mission comes to fruition.

GLOBALIZATION

Globalization is another critical trend that will impact how ministry organizations and their leaders engage, interact, and do ministry. The world is becoming more interconnected and cosmopolitan. This trend is also affecting the church. The implications for this trend, as it relates to leadership, means as globalization continues to bring tremendous changes in the world, organizations will be challenged to raise the bar in leadership.[29] It is paramount to develop Gen-X and Millennial leaders that have the necessary skills and competencies to engage global cultures. This begins with ministry leaders recapturing the global dimension of the Great Commission, equipping believers to think

---

[26]Allen, J.L. (2009). *The future church: How ten trends are revolutionizing the church.* New York, NY: Crown Publishing.
[27]Ibid.
[28]Cameron, K.S. & Quinn, R.E. (2011). *Diagnosing and changing organizational culture.* San Francisco, CA: Jossey-Bass.
[29]Hines, A. (2006). "Strategic Foresight: The State of the Art." Futurist, 40(5), 18-21.

globally, and establishing partnership for cross-cultural ministry, which will give individuals the opportunity to work in multicultural teams.[30]

MENTAL MODELS

As these driving forces are considered, change is essential in order to remain relevant moving forward. To spark change in an organization, one must address mental models and paradigm shifts. Mental models are representations of reality that people use to understand and analyze how structures work. The models represent deeply ingrained assumptions or generalizations that influence how we understand the world and how we take action.[31]

Leaders often get locked into a mindset by which they tend to filter out information that does not fit their current paradigm. In order to avoid this, leaders must break old paradigms and step outside of preconceived mental models to keep up with an ever-changing reality.[32] When mental models are left unchallenged, organizations will see what they have always seen.

Organizations need to be learning organizations where employees continually expand their capacities to create results they truly desire, where new and expansive patterns of thinking are nurtured, where collective aspiration is set free, and where people are collaborating and learning together.[33] To create a new reality that is different than the past, leaders should move away from "low-hanging fruit" and change to higher orders of thinking and understanding. To find sustainable solutions in an ever-changing world, leaders must be able to endure the development of innovative strategies to deal with an unfolding reality.

As a Christian coach and one that has served in secular and church leadership positions, it is important for leaders to understand how powerful mental models and paradigm shifts are. I have experienced firsthand in the finance/audit industry how paramount it is to empower people to be free to think and take ownership and commitment for decisions. As a new business initiative, my team and I were tasked by

---

[30]Gibbons, S. (2010). "The Covenant Leader: Leading Faithfully." *Inner Resources for Leaders*, 2(3), 1-9.
[31]Clark, T.R. (2005). *A Mouse of Change, a Lion of Resistance*.
[32]Glick, M.B., Chermack, T.J., Luckel, H., & Gauck, B.Q. (2012). "Effects of Scenario Planning on Participant Mental Models." *European Journal of Training and Development*, 36(5), 488-507.
[33]Allee, V. (1997). *The Knowledge Evolution: Expanding Organizational Intelligence*. Newton, MA: Focal Press.

senior leadership to devise ways to innovate my organization's finance department. I set weekly synergy meetings, coaching my team to create ongoing conversations of needs, opportunities, tasks, and projects to build an innovative environment for the department. These synergy meetings helped shift the mental models and paradigms of the team to think innovatively, grow their skills, and test strategies for execution.

As a coaching leader, it was critical to create an encouraging and supportive environment for futuristic thinking. As a result, the team and I were successful in birthing new practices, processes, and technologies that captured data and metrics that provided actionable insights for new ways to do business financially.

READY, SET, GO!

Change-oriented mindsets are the wave of the future. Leaders managing organizational change should be able to see all systems, to look at the moving pieces in a way that is logical, complete, and comprehensive.[34] They think holistically regarding strategy, organizational capabilities, work, structure, and process. Driving lasting change means working *through* people in the organization instead of working *around* them. As masters of change, these leaders have the ability to scan their business market, revamp their strategies, and act on those strategies.[35]

Jay Gary, a futurist expert, shares our world is rapidly changing to the point where traditional planning based on budgets and program review is no longer sufficient in itself to propel your organization into the future.[36] Scanning the horizon and reframing issues are two ways to turn from static strategic planning to dynamic strategic foresight. Some non-profits are turning to scenario planning to further stress test their plans. The important thing is to begin the journey upstream to spawn long-term creativity and innovation, rather than just target near-term, downstream results. This may not cure you losing sleep over whether your business model is future ready, but at least you will

---

[34] Haake, D. (2015). "Out of the Box, into the Scenario." *Planning, 78*(10), 40-43.
[35] Wilkinson, A. & Kupers, R. (2013). "Living in the Futures: How Scenario Planning Changed Corporate Strategy." *Harvard Business Review, 91*(5), 118-127.
[36] Gary, J.E. (2010). "*Strategic Foresight: Looking to the Future to Play Today.*" Outcomes **Magazine**, 34(2), 26-27.

generate a way for your strategic team to make the journey with you.[37]

QUESTIONS FOR CONSIDERATION:

1. Strategic foresight is meant to shape our organizations. Where have you been afraid to stop and assess your progress for the wave of the future?

2. As you scan your organization and the driving forces of change in the current environment, are there areas that necessitate a pivot and redirection?

---

[37] Ibid.

III GEN Y Z

CHAPTER 3:

GENERATION X VS. MILLENNIALS

Many employers could have employees ranging from the ages of 18 to 80 in today's workplace. This has huge implications for organizations in terms of managing the needs and expectations of multiple generations, as is the case with Millennials and Generation X'ers. Picture the scene: You have a fresh-faced graduate working alongside a forty-year-old colleague on the same project. These two employees work for the same organization but have contrasting expectations and views of the workplace.

This same notion holds true for church organizations. The baton of leadership within ministries should be passed smoothly, and Millennials should rise on the strength of Gen-X leadership. At the same time, church organizations should be cognizant of incorporating Millennials and their array of skillsets without alienating Generation X or other generations.

THE MULTIGENERATIONAL WORKFORCE[38]

Here are the characteristics of each generation in today's workforce:

TRADITIONALISTS – BORN 1925 TO 1945

This group is considered among the most loyal workers. They are highly dedicated and the most risk averse. The Great Depression, World War II, and the postwar boom years shaped their values. They possess a strong commitment to teamwork and collaboration, and have high regard for developing interpersonal communication skills. They now consist of the most affluent elderly population in US history due to their willingness to conserve and save after recovering from the financial impact of the postwar era.

BABY BOOMERS – BORN 1946 TO 1964

Boomers are the first generation to actively declare a higher priority for work over personal life. They generally distrust authority and large systems. Their values were shaped primarily by a rise in civil rights activism, Vietnam, and inflation. They are more optimistic and open

---
[38] Delcampo, R.G., Haggerty, L.A., Haney, M.J., Knippel, L.A. (2016). *Managing the multi-generational workforce: From the GI generation to the millennials.* New York, NY: Routledge.

to change than the prior generation, but they are also responsible for the "Me Generation," with its pursuit of personal gratification, which often shows up as a sense of entitlement in today's work force.

GENERATION X'ERS – BORN 1965 TO 1980

This group is often considered the "slacker" generation. They have a tendency to question authority figures and are responsible for creating the work-life balance concept. Born in a time of declining population growth, this generation of workers possess strong technical skills and are more independent than the prior generations. Because Gen X'ers, in general, place a lower priority on work, many company leaders from the Baby Boomer generation assume these workers are not as dedicated. However, Gen X'ers are willing to develop their skill sets and take on new challenges. They are perceived as very adaptive to job instability in the post-downsizing environment.

MILLENNIALS – BORN 1981 TO 2000

This group is the first global-centric generation, having come of age during the rapid growth of the internet and an increase in global terrorism. They are among the most resilient in navigating change while deepening their appreciation for diversity and inclusion. With significant gains in technology and an increase in educational programming during the 1990s, the Millennials are also the most educated generation of workers today. Additionally, they represent the most team-centric generation since the Traditionalists, as they have grown up at a time where parents programmed much of their lives with sports, music, and recreational activities to keep them occupied, while their Boomer parents focused on work.

DIFFERENCES BETWEEN GEN X'ERS AND MILLENNIALS[39]

---

[39]Buckley, P., Viechnicki, P. & Barua, A. (2015). "A New Understanding of Millennials: Generational Differences Reexamined." Retrieved from https://www2.deloitte.com/insights/us/en/economy/issues-by-the-numbers/understanding-millennials-generational-differences.html

DISTINCTIVES OF GEN X'ERS:

- Gen X'ers are independent, resourceful, and self-sufficient. They value freedom, adapt well to change, and accept responsibility in organizations. They have a casual disdain for authority and structured work hours.

- They dislike being micro-managed and embrace a hands-off management philosophy.

- They value hard work, are ambitious, and are eager to learn new skills. They appreciate fun in organizations and have a work hard/play hard mentality.

- They define themselves by their accomplishments.

- They emphasize teamwork and enjoy regular face-to-face meetings.

- They tend to be less committed to a single employer. They are dedicated and welcome challenging projects to make a difference.

- They criticize Millennials for a lack of work ethic and commitment to the workplace.

- They are motivated by power, positions, perks, and prestige.

DISTINCTIVES OF MILLENNIALS:[40]

- Millennials are continuous learners, team players, and diverse collaborators who are optimistic, achievement oriented, socially conscious, and highly educated. They are real, confident, social, and love to have fun.

---

[40] Harber, Jeffery G., *"Generations in the Workplace: Similarities and Differences."* (2011). Electronic Theses and Dissertations. Paper 1255. http://dc.etsu.edu/etd/1255

- They enjoy virtual meetings as opposed to face-to-face meetings.

- They seek employability and flexibility. Work is not just about income; it is about personal enrichment and fulfillment.

- They want to trust in their organization's leadership, receive benefits, and obtain professional development opportunities.

- They pride themselves on being holistic, sensible, responsible, and genuinely concerned about their society and community.

- They long for leadership development programs that are coaching driven. They recognize coaching helps to develop competencies and self-awareness to become more effective and reflective.

- Millennials crave attention, feedback, and praise; they accept guidance from experienced coaches or mentors.

- They are tenacious multitaskers that are goal oriented. They love to be empowered collaborators.

Generation X'ers grew up with computers and lived through the development of the internet. As the first latchkey kids, they learned how to be independent at an early age. After seeing widespread layoffs of workaholic parents, this generation has a marked desire for work-life balance and resists being workaholics.

AS FAR AS LEARNING, GEN X'ERS:[41]

- Prefer to learn by doing.

---

[41]Reeves, T.C. & Oh, E. (2015). Generational Differences. Retrieved from http://www.aect.org/edtech/edition3/ER5849x_C025.fm.pdf

- Prefer independent, self-directed learning, including individual research or projects.

- Admire the build-in of activities at work *(field trips, debates, role-play, and games)*.

- Prefer the use of technology where possible, including online training and testing.

- Prefer immediate feedback.

- Desire support materials available after training.

- Will turn to a computer before books.

- Like the freedom to figure out things on their own—to come up with answers and alternatives.

- See training as career security and a plus for the job market.

- Like having a say in the work and leadership content.

Millennials, on the other hand, have grown up in the internet years and its accelerated pace of development. They are accustomed to multitasking and can be effective at it. Although much of their social life is conducted online, they do prefer collaborative, team-oriented environments.

MILLENNIALS PREFER:[42]

- Learning environments with peer interactions.

- Reinforcement and reaffirmation.

- Fast-moving, interactive activities.

---

[42] Ibid.

- Short and sweet learning, not patient for lengthy lectures and endless PPT presentations.

- Entertainment and learning at the same time.

- Technology over everything.

- Their smartphones as resources.

- Clear learning paths and clear expectations.

- Direct benefits to be clear for motivation. If it's not, they become disinterested.

- Education and leadership development, which is a direct link to advancing their careers to make more money.

SIMILARITIES BETWEEN GEN X'ERS AND MILLENNIALS

First things first, it's important to recognize that both generations have a pretty big thing in common: They both want to be shown respect. Gen X'ers crave respect and acknowledgment from younger workers, and Millennials generally feel they deserve recognition in the workplace—regardless of their age or level of experience.

Beyond that, Millennials and Gen X'ers can complement each other well in a work setting, filling in the gaps to create a diverse and accomplished team. For example, Millennials who are new to the workforce will require a certain amount of direction and supervision. Gen X'ers, who are exceptionally skilled at delegating assignments, can easily fall into this role and provide instruction to their younger counterparts.

Both generations have similar values of teamwork and flexible work arrangements. Each generation shares the need for work-life balance and desire time to spend with their family and friends. Likewise, both generations are motivated by meaning and customization of careers, where they seek and prefer jobs that challenge them and have rewarding experiences.

Both Millennials and Gen X'ers are devoted to development because they desire to be a part of an organization that provides continual training and development opportunities. Millennials have a strong appetite for professional development when they enter the workplace and it continues to grow as they rise into leadership positions inside of organizations. Generation X'ers are committed to continuous learning and development because they are aware of having to learn at greater levels to maximize their careers. They both understand that education and leadership development is the direct link to advancing their careers and being financially rewarded for their work.

Coaching in organizations also compels both generations. In fact, coaching is the workplace leadership style that resonates with Millennials. Generation X'ers also pursue coaching relationships because they desire leaders to coach them through learning, decisions, and actions that affect their work. Remember the story I shared in Chapter Two about leading a team to innovate the processes and technologies of the finance department where I worked? To dig deeper, this team was made up of a mix of Millennials and Gen X'ers. As the coach, I was privileged and willing to exercise my leadership and add value to create a synergistic atmosphere where both groups were empowered to make decisions, share information, and try new things. The reason why the team was successful is that both groups had ownership in creating a favorable environment to develop and grow their skills professionally as an innovative team. These same factors are what will empower those from different generations to work together in a synergistic capacity toward the successful accomplishment of organizational goals.

With a clear picture of the distinctions and similarities of Millennials and Gen X'ers, now is a great time for reflection. Contemplate the differences and similarities outlined in this chapter by considering the following questions:

1. What drives/motivates the members of each generation in your organizations?

2. Can you think of how you have seen this to be true in your unique contexts?

3. What are ways you can help provide motivating work environments and interactions based on these similarities and differences represented on your team?

IV

CHAPTER 4:

LEADERSHIP STYLES

The future of work centers on the significance of the Millennial generation, as they are the largest segment of the US workforce and will dominate the landscape for decades to come. In order to ensure effective Millennial leadership development, the future calls for Gen X'ers and Millennials to partner in multigenerational work environments. Since organizations have both generations in leadership, it is important to learn about leadership styles and how they affect the workplace. Leaders and the style in which they function have a direct cause and effect relationship upon organizations and their success. Whether a Gen-X or Millennial leader in church or a business organization, leaders determine values, culture, change tolerance, and people motivation. Likewise, leaders shape institutional strategies, which include their execution and effectiveness.

The advantage to understanding your leadership style is that this awareness will in turn help you understand your strengths and weaknesses. Leadership awareness can help you become proactive and more effective as a leader by strategically leveraging your strengths to counteract your weaker areas. Your leadership style defines your values and perspective. Knowing your leadership style empowers you to move forward as an influential leader in your organization.

TRANSFORMATIONAL LEADERSHIP

Transformational leaders create an extraordinary vision for their organizations, one which employees are then eager to fully "buy into" and work incredibly hard every day to bring it to life.[43] What's more, transformational leaders are obsessed about developing their people, not merely collecting a profit. To put it simply, transformational leaders positively disrupt individual organizations and entire industries.

AUTHENTIC LEADERSHIP

George describes authentic leadership as a leadership style consistent with a leader's personality, core values, honesty, and ethics.[44] In organizations, leaders oftentimes are pressured to "play the role"

---

[43] McCleskey, J.A. (2014). *"Situational, Transformational, and Transactional Leadership and Leadership Development."* Journal of Business Studies Quarterly, 5(4), 117-130.

[44] George, B. (2010). *True North: Discover Your Authentic Leadership.* New York, NY: Wiley.

and end up changing themselves to fit in with other leaders and colleagues. This leaves followers feeling as if their leaders are being deceitful, which leads to mistrust and turnover in organizations.[45] Conversely, when leaders are authentic in their leadership approach, they are trusted as real, effective, productive, and inspiring.

Authenticity means being genuine—not a replica, a copy, or an imitation. As a leader, we must embody our true authentic self in our leadership roles. Being true to ourselves calls us to draw on the very essence of our values, beliefs, principles, and morals as our guiding compass.[46] This means we find our strengths while recognizing our weaknesses and taking accountability for the way our leadership impacts others.

So, let's dive into characteristics of authentic leadership:[47]

Self-Awareness – Authentic leaders make mistakes but are willing to admit their errors and learn from them. They know how to ask others for help. Because of that, authentic leaders are humble and able to lead through difficult situations.

Integral – Being real and genuine is the way to go! Face it, people can sense quickly if a leader is truly authentic. Leaders who lack authenticity will not gain the trust of those they lead. When leaders are integral, followers will respond very positively to requests for help when difficult times arise.

Growth – Authentic leaders are constantly in a state of development as they learn and grow from their experiences. Just as athletes train for great performances, authentic leaders practice to be great leaders. They are continuously evolving as they empower and inspire others.

Emotional Intelligence – Leaders who are emotionally intelligent do not burst out with what they may be thinking or

---

[45]Ibid.
[46]Mundahl, S. (2013). *The Alchemy of Authentic Leadership.* Bloomington, IN: Balboa Press.
[47]George, B. (2003). *Authentic Leadership: Rediscovering the Secrets to Creating Lasting Value.* New York, NY: Wiley.

feeling. They exhibit self-control, understand how they may be perceived as leaders, and use emotional intelligence to communicate with those they lead.

Insight – Soldiers in King David's army "understood the times and knew what Israel should do" (1 Chronicles 12:32). Authentic leaders operate in wisdom and discernment for the present and future. They have the necessary insight to reboot, gain clarity, and determine courses of action that help themselves and others.

SERVANT LEADERSHIP

While servant leadership is a timeless concept, the phrase "servant leadership" was originally coined by Robert K. Greenleaf in *The Servant as Leader*, an essay he first published in 1970. In that essay, Greenleaf said,

The servant-leader is servant first… It begins with the natural feeling that one wants to serve, to serve first. Then, conscious choice brings one to aspire to lead. That person is sharply different from one who is leader first, perhaps because of the need to assuage an unusual power drive or to acquire material possessions…The leader-first and the servant-first are two extreme types. Between them, there are shadings and blends that are part of the infinite variety of human nature.[48]

A servant-leader focuses primarily on the growth and well-being of people and the communities to which they belong. While traditional leadership generally involves the accumulation and exercise of power by one at the "top of the pyramid," servant leadership is different. The servant-leader shares power, puts the needs of others first, and helps people develop and perform as highly as possible.

CHARACTERISTICS OF SERVANT LEADERS

The following are characteristics of servant leaders:[49]

---

[48] Greenleaf, Robert. (1970). *The Servant as Leader*. South Orange, NJ: The Greenleaf Center for Servant Leadership.
[49] Spears, L.C. (2005). *The Understanding and Practice of Servant Leadership*. Retrieved from https://www.regent.edu/acad/global/publications/sl_proceedings/2005/spears_practice.pdf

Listening – Servant leaders commit to listen intently to others. They listen to what is being said and unsaid. Listening, coupled with periods of reflection, is essential to the growth and well-being of the servant leader.

Empathy – Servant leaders seek to understand and empathize with others. People need to be accepted and recognized for their uniqueness. The most successful servant leaders are those who have become skilled, empathetic listeners.

Healing – Servant leaders are transformative people that recognize they have an opportunity to help people they lead to become whole. They often help people that have been broken in their spirits and have suffered many emotional hurts to find healing.

Self-Awareness – The leadership quality of self-awareness strengthens servant leaders. It helps leaders to understand issues such as ethics, power, and values. Self-awareness lends itself to being able to help leaders view most situations from a more integrated, holistic position.

Foresight – Earlier in the chapter, we covered strategic foresight. This is a critical leadership quality to possess. Servant leaders have intuitive minds that understand the lessons of the past, the realities of the present, and the preferred future.

Commitment to the Transformation of People – Servant leaders believe people have an intrinsic value beyond their tangible contributions as workers. As such, the servant leader is deeply committed to the growth of each and every individual within his or her organization. The servant leader recognizes the tremendous responsibility to do everything in his or her power to nurture the personal and professional growth of employees and colleagues. In practice, this can include (but is not limited to) concrete actions such as making funds available for personal and professional development, taking a personal interest in ideas and suggestions from everyone, and encouraging worker involvement in decision-making.

Building Community – The servant leader understands much has been lost in recent human history as a result of the shift from local communities to large institutions as the primary shaper of human lives. This awareness causes the servant leader to seek to identify means for building community among those who work within a given institution. Servant leadership suggests true community can be created among those who work in businesses and other institutions.

STRATEGIC LEADERSHIP

Strategic leadership speaks to a leader's potential to express and realize a determined vision for their organization, while motivating and persuading others to acquire that vision. Strategic leaders execute organizational change and make great use of reward and incentive systems for encouraging productivity and performance.[50] Strategic leadership means they think, act, and influence purposefully. These leaders are strategic thinkers who understand the complex relationship between the organization and its environment, take decisive action consistent with the strategic direction of the organization, and build commitment to their organization's direction by inviting others to the strategic process.[51]

Here are a few examples of organizations who missed the opportunity to implement strategic leadership in their organizational approach:

BlackBerry – This tech company launched in 1999 and rose quickly to the top due to their star product, BlackBerry smartphones. The company, which controlled 50 percent

---
[50] Leitch, J., Lancefield, D. & Dawson, M. (2016). *10 Principles of Strategic Leadership*. Strategy +Business, 84.
[51] Ibid.

of the smartphone market, unfortunately did not innovate, however, when the other competitors of the smartphone age arrived on the scene. The organization fell out of touch with what was happening around them and failed to change with the coming trends. BlackBerry was weakened and paralyzed by organizational threats and new growth opportunities.[52]

Borders – This organization made the mistake of outsourcing its online book selling to Amazon. The relinquishing of control hurt Borders' branding strategies and cut into its customer base. At the same time, Borders was too late to launch e-books, opened too many stores, had too much debt, and over-invested in music sales.[53]

Blockbuster – At the pinnacle of Blockbuster's success, the company began to alienate their customers with strict late fees and unimaginative, warehouse-style stores.[54] Additionally, the organization overlooked e-commerce by sticking to its long-standing retail strategy. Just think—Blockbuster at one time had the opportunity to purchase Netflix yet decided against the acquisition!

Although each of these scenarios are unique, the common thread within each example is that these organizations failed to employ strategic leadership in their organizations when it mattered the most. As a result, their lack of strategic leadership and ability to pivot with the changing times left them vulnerable to external threats. BlackBerry, Borders, and Blockbuster all became irrelevant and missed opportunities to innovate, causing the demise of their operations.

Now, let's talk about organizations that have leveraged strategic leadership to maximize their potential:

---

[52]Gustin, S. (2013). *The Fatal Mistake That Doomed BlackBerry*. Retrieved from http://business.time.com/2013/09/24/the-fatal-mistake-that-doomed-blackberry/
[53]Wall, M. (2014). "Innovate or Die: The Stark Message for Big Business." Retrieved from http://www.bbc.com/news/business-28865268
[54]Ibid.

Unilever – This innovative organization has been a global leader with well-known brands that make beverages, food, cleaning agents, and personal care products. Unilever prides itself on brands that combine superior experiences, bold innovation, and a strong, sustainable living purpose. Unilever has an ambitious, long-term strategy to transform its growth model to reduce environmental impact and make sustainable living commonplace. They have strategies in place to create robust solutions that deal with global nutrition, the shower of the future, and even reinventing laundry to be less water intensive.[55] Unilever crafted their brand messages with relevant and inspiring messages during the coronavirus pandemic shelter-in-place orders. Their brand messages have spoken to events such as things to stay inspired, home barbecuing, and summer staycations. As a result, the organization accelerated in its e-commerce sales and new branding opportunities to introduce to people adjusting to life under pandemic conditions.

Tesla – This American electric vehicle and clean energy organization, founded in 2003, has made a disruptive impact in the automotive industry. Elon Musk, CEO of the organization, has consistently encouraged technological developments in all of its projects and partnerships. Tesla has disrupted the way we think about energy storage and sustainable futures.[56] Tesla recently diversified its brand into solar panel and solar roof tile manufacturing for homes. This innovative approach to the changing times is a telltale marker of an organization who will continue to make its mark well into the future.

Amazon – This multinational technology company has positioned itself as the world's largest online marketplace and live-streaming platform. Amazon has emphasized platforms to

---

[55] Makower, J. (2012). *"Why Unilever is Betting on Open Innovation for Sustainability."* Retrieved from https://www.greenbiz.com/blog/2012/03/29/why-unilever-placing-its-sustainability-bets-open-innovation
[56] Nicholson, D. (2014). *"Inside Tesla – A Rare Glimpse of Electric Carmaker's Culture."* Retrieved from https://www.forbes.com/sites/davidnicholson/2014/11/09/inside-tesla-a-rare-glimpse-of-electric-carmakers-culture/#2bd558c47ffb

serve its own customers in fast and efficient ways. Since 1994, Amazon has built strategies of continuous evolution that have allowed the company to experiment in adjacent areas, building them into franchises.[57] Their new Seattle fulfillment center has high-tech robots working alongside human workers like a factory of the future. In 2017, Amazon expanded its footprint as a physical retailer by acquiring Whole Foods Market for $13.4 billion.

These three organizations are examples of how to strategically lead into the future. Although these are secular organizations, **church organizations need this same level of strategic leadership as well**! So, let's explore the main characteristics of effective strategic leaders that create superior performance, innovation, and creativity.

STRATEGIC LEADERS ARE EMOTIONALLY INTELLIGENT

In today's world of instant results and self-gratification, humility and emotional intelligence are essential leadership attributes often lacking among contemporary leaders. According to Angel Cabrera and Gregory Unruh, for a strategic leader, mastery of emotional intelligence (EI) is essential for the fluidity of engagement, motivation, and inspiration when working with individuals of various cultures.[58] Fluency in EI enables leaders to stop, listen, and understand how to adjust their leadership for their employees to get the desired result. After all, employees are the conduits where innovative and creative improvements are achieved regarding work, performance, and immediate solutions to problems while sharing information and ideas through informal, social, and collaborative interaction.[59]

STRATEGIC LEADERS ARE BUILDERS OF EXCELLENT TEAMS

Paul Kirkbride notes "innovative leaders articulate, in an exciting

---

[57] Robischon, N. (2017). *"Why Amazon Is the World's Most Innovative Company of 2017."* Retrieved from https://www.fastcompany.com/3067455/why-amazon-is-the-worlds-most-innovative-company-of-2017

[58] Cabrera, A. & Unruh, G. (2012). *Being Global: How to Think, Act, and Lead in a Transformed World.* Boston, MA: Harvard Business Review Press.

[59] Ibid.

and compelling manner, a vision of the future that followers can accept and strive towards."[60] Additionally, innovative leaders actively lead global teams in sharing knowledge and experiences that are characterized by mutual sharing, respect, diversity, participation, and transformations, which occur through high-order thinking and communication. Leadership expert Peter G. Northouse asserts innovative leaders set out to empower followers and nurture them to change. These types of leaders raise the consciousness in individuals and help them to transcend their self-interests for the sake of others. In addition to this, innovative leaders build trust and collaboration while bringing out the best in their followers for the greater common good."[61]

Today's leaders of organizations should encourage the spirit of innovation and creativity by establishing working environments that create disruptive and incremental innovation, fostering teamwork and collaboration. Paula Caligiuri states, "leaders that ask for input in decision-making stimulate communication, buy-in, and innovative ideas to facilitate a positive cultural move for the future."[62] Scott Berkun stresses the fact that:

> *Leaders should foster a culture that generates trust and encourages information exchange that promotes the successful execution of strategy, continual change, innovation, employee buy-in, and results that create better ways of doing business. When trust and information exchange are present in organizations, new mental models of innovation are the catalyst that can propel organizations into a viable future.*[63]

STRATEGIC LEADERS HAVE INTEGRITY

Integrity within leadership goes a long way in organizations! Morgan W. McCall and George Hollenbeck wrote:

---

[60]Kirkbride, P. (2006). Developing "Transformational Leaders: The Full Range Leadership Model in Action." *Industrial and Commercial Training. 38*(1), 23-32.
[61]Northouse, P.G. (2016). *Leadership: Theory and Practice*. Thousand Oaks, CA: Sage.
[62]Caligiuri, P. (2012). *Cultural Agility: Building a Pipeline of Successful Global Professionals*. New York, NY: Wiley.
[63]Berkun, S. (2008). *Making Things Happen: Mastering Project Management*. Boston, MA: O'Reilly.

Leaders can shape the corporate soul and culture of organizations by being ethical, with a strong set of people-centered values. This speaks volumes to their followers, from their demonstration of respect, fairness, kindness, and honesty. Their ethical influence will influence others to lead ethically as well.[64]

Since ethics and values are the glue that holds organizations together, Georges Enderle and Patrick E. Murphy discuss that there is a need for "leaders to live up to the values and ethics that they say they believe to make ethical behavior a priority."[65] For the public sector, the private sector, and ecclesial organizations to perform at an optimal level, their ethical infrastructures must be aligned with their strategies and core values. Since the ethical behavior and values of leaders permeate everything in the business environment, leaders have a responsibility to make a declaration of their organization's ethical stance to establish an innovative and creative working culture that is values based. When this occurs, innovative leaders are effective, inspiring, and communicate to their followers that ethical behavior is paramount to organizational success.

STRATEGIC LEADERS ARE CATALYSTS

Innovative leaders are self-disciplined, carefully meeting deadlines and commitments to produce opportunities and solutions that are done right the first time. As methodical catalysts, innovative leaders are self-disciplined in scanning the environment and identifying global doors. They have organizational aptitude and experience with direct knowledge of organizational matters. In the face of adversity, they are courageous to risk failing and learn from failure. As methodical thinkers, they can drive innovation in the midst of challenges. Via self-discipline, these leaders are mature, consistent, rational thinkers that demonstrate strong decision-making to show their followers their willingness to do what is needed for the organization versus what

---

[64]McCall, M.W. & Hollenbeck, G. (2002). *Developing Global Executives*. Boston, MA: Harvard Business School Press.
[65]Murphy, P.E. & Enderle, G. (1995). "Managerial Ethical Leadership." *Business Ethics Quarterly*. 5(1), 117-128.

they desire.[66]

Creating a culture of discipline is a must to sustain innovation across entire organizations. To drive high performance, leaders and organizations must educate their employees regarding the dynamics of innovation and reward behavior that leads to creative and innovative ideas.[67] This leads to innovative outcomes that ultimately drive organizational growth and performance.

THEY ARE INNOVATIVE THINKERS

Adam Gordon, an expert consultant in the field of strategic foresight and management, speaks of analytical focus for strategic execution of great ideas. He states:

> *Setting strategy and performance expectations helps identify trends to make better decisions to execute innovative ideas for excellent outcomes. The organization's strategic plan is all about setting up ways for people to bring their innovative thinking to the surface, sparking learning outcomes to make the most of their creativity for marketplace impact.*[68]

This means leaders have to disconnect from idea killers that hinder innovation. Scott Berkun says idea killers consist of:

> *...the 'we tried that already mentality,' which hinders the discovery of exceptional ideas. Leaders must be willing to explore, experiment, and play to invest energy, hit a dead end, and then chase a new direction that allows minds to find good ideas.*[69]

---

[66] Ibid.
[67] Gleeson, B. (2017). "Why Creating a Culture of Discipline Is the Path to Greatness." Retrieved from https://www.inc.com/brent-gleeson/why-creating-a-culture-of-discipline-is-the-path-t.html
[68] Gordon, A. (2008). *Future Savvy: Identifying Trends to Make Better Decisions, Manage Uncertainty, and Profit for Change.* New York, NY: AMACOM.
[69] Berkun, S. (2008). *Making Things Happen: Mastering Project Management.* Boston, MA: O'Reilly.

From there, leaders forge forward with strategic planning and execution to look across industries and scrutinize the activities of their competitors. They focus and uncover business and industry trends to incorporate change and innovation in the services and products their organizations offer.

Creating channels for innovative ideas guides the future alignment opportunity strategies for the benefit of the organization. Their innovative ideas help leaders to consider future-anticipating forecasts that uncover what products to create and what markets to develop to profit from the future changes to their industries. Thomas H. Davenport, Jeanne G. Harris, and Robert Morison argue that big picture thinking "illuminates demographic shifts, economic trends, and changes in what customers and clients want. This type of thinking uncovers exploring 'intuitive hunches about the business and where the next breakthrough may await.'"[70] Leaders create channels of innovation by assembling cross-functional forums where people can present ideas and test them against the group.

Coaching and leadership development programs create teams of promising thinkers that spark conversation by encouraging interaction among employees and leaders in various departments.[71] Although conversations may be challenging due to uncertainty, leaders working with their employees across the organization will raise the strategic value of creating and sustaining an innovative environment. Channels of innovative ideas will then birth future transformation for organizational progression.

The influence of strategic leaders within an organization is essential to succeeding in today's business world. Without individuals to inspire action, anticipate challenges, seek organizational feedback, and evaluate data, organizations will have a challenging time moving in the right direction.

CROSS-CULTURAL LEADERSHIP

Cross-cultural leadership is important for organizations, especially in today's global environment. Since one of the most critical elements

---

[70] Davenport, T.H., Harris, J.G. and Morison, R. (2010). *Analytics at Work: Smarter Decisions, Better Results.* Boston, MA: Harvard Business Review.
[71] Battley, S. (2007). *Coached to Lead.* San Francisco, CA: Jossey-Bass.

of any organization involve how leaders think, act, and lead globally, leaders must deal with diverse cultures to maintain agility in our rapidly changing world. The move toward a cross-cultural global marketplace sparks the need for leaders to possess and activate a global mindset to develop the skills, competencies, and awareness of how culture affects their leadership. If leaders do not lead cross-culturally, in the long run, it can prove to be a hindrance to productivity, stagnating growth, creativity, and innovation.

SO, WHAT ARE CHARACTERISTICS OF CROSS-CULTURAL LEADERS?

GLOBAL MINDSET

A global mindset is the ability to lead and rapidly react to changes while managing complex, interpersonal relationships in order to reach excellence amid ambiguity driven by cultural differences in organizational values, patterns, attitudes, and behaviors.[72] Leaders with global mindsets lead with curiosity and seek to understand themselves and the world around them. Their life experiences are the catalyst of continual leadership development. Leaders that possess a global mindset are most successful in today's global business environments because they aspire to be lifelong learners with an affinity for diversity.

GLOBAL PSYCHOLOGICAL CAPITAL

Leaders with significant global psychological capital have the cognitive ability to analyze situations from multiple, even competing, points of view. One emergent trend is cultural intelligence or cultural quotient in global business environments.

Cultural intelligence is defined as a leader's capability to function effectively across national, ethnic, and organizational cultures. Interactions in the global workplace require individuals to be capable of managing the merging of today's world, being sensitive to diverse cultures, analyzing cultures, understanding the requirements of people from other cultures, and engaging in appropriate interactions with them.[73] To be effective, culturally intelligent global leaders who engage

[72]Steffey, D. (2017). "Do You Have a Global Mindset?" Retrieved from https://www.td.org/insights/do-you-have-a-global-mindset
[73]Clapp-Smith, R., Luthans, F. & Avolio, B.J. (2007). "The Role of Psychological Capital in Global Mindset Development." *Advances in*

their followers need leadership development in observation, empathy, and intelligence to interpret situations for decision-making.

GLOBAL INTELLECTUAL CAPITAL

The development of global intellectual capital breeds cosmopolitan leaders who dedicate their time and effort to learning about economic and political issues, along with the complexities of international affairs from multiple national perspectives.[74] With an increasingly borderless world, organizations must build leaders who understand and embrace the cultural, regulatory, political, and personal nuances prevalent in their workforce and the markets they serve.

To thrive in a global marketplace, leaders must also be able to see past cultural biases to become strategically adaptable and operationally efficient to manage various ways of working with diverse cultures.[75] One specific way for organizations to help their leaders develop global competencies/cross-cultural leadership is by establishing global leadership training programs which cultivate cross-cultural teams. One strategy to build virtual, multicultural team collaborations enables global members to learn about each other to foster cultural synergy. From these partnerships, the culture of organizations evolves to enable diverse teams to collectively engage in behaviors that support strategy and contribute to great organizational performance.[76]

GLOBAL SOCIAL CAPITAL

Leaders who major on global social capital display an unusual ability to connect emotionally and communicate effectively with individuals from various cultural backgrounds. Leaders with global mindsets are apt to build global social capital by establishing and sharing connections to enable the flow of knowledge, collaboration, information, and resources.[77] Global leaders should embrace cross-

---

International Management, 19, 105-130.
[74]Ibid.
[75]Beechler, S. & Woodward, I.C. (2009). "The Global War for Talent." *Journal of International Management, 15,* 273-285.
[76]Ibid.
[77]Osland, J. S., Oddou, G., Bird, A. & Osland, A. (2013). "Exceptional Global Leadership as Cognitive Expertise in the Domain of Global Change." *European Journal of International Management, 7,* 517-534

cultural diversity, connecting with other cultures by communicating and building trust to build credibility to work effectively in cross-cultural jobs, tasks, and roles. One strategy leaders can employ to bridge the cultural gap is to create diverse teams. The remedy for these gaps would be for leaders to create teams of different ages and cultures for profitable collaboration. Diverse teams create rich learning opportunities across cultures and generations in organizations and harmonious teamwork toward organizational goals.[78]

COACHING LEADERSHIP

Coaching has become a buzzword in organizations when discussing leadership development. Eighty-six percent of organizations believe coaching is needed for the future of their organizations but do not leverage leadership development and coaching for future growth.[79] The world of business and ministry is rapidly changing daily, which means organizations must prepare for future trends in order to stay relevant. If organizations do not prepare effectively, it can spell disaster for your operational performance down the road.

This is why the coaching leadership style is important! Coaching has successfully evolved from fad to fundamental since its introduction to the business world decades ago. How can coaching leadership help your organization? According to Shanta Harper, coaching adds value to organizations by enhancing the quality of leaders. The adoption of coaching is a sustainable strategy for human capital development and organization enhancement.[80] Coaching leaders creates value by helping organizations focus on growing the emotional and relational aspects of leadership capacities.

With this in mind, what do coaching leaders actually do for their organizations? You will certainly encounter change ahead! Let's take a few minutes to discuss how coaches impact organizations.

Coaches Increase Effectiveness: Coaching leaders broaden

---

[78]Ibid.
[79]Hall, D.T., Otazo, K.L., & Hollenbeck, G.P. (1999). "Behind Closed Doors: What Really Happens in Executive Coaching." *Organizational Dynamics*, 27(3), 39-53.
[80]Harper, S. (2012). The leader coach: A model of multi-style leadership. *Journal of Practical Consulting*, 4(1), 22-31.

thinking, identify strengths and developmental needs, and set and achieve challenging goals.

Coaches Build Relationships: Coaching leaders establish healthy relational connections through building trust. They provide clarity about the learning and development objectives they set, show good judgment, are patient, and follow through on any promises and agreements that they make.[81]

Coaches Utilize the Power of Assessments: Assessments uncover valuable information, such as "Where are you now? And where do you desire to go?" Coaching leaders help others gain self-awareness and insight through the use of these assessments. They provide timely feedback and help identify the behaviors people would like to change. Assessments focus on gaps or inconsistencies, current performance vs. desired performance, words vs. actions, and intention vs. impact.[82]

Coaches Challenge Thinking and Assumptions: Coaching shifts paradigms and mental models of leaders to lead themselves and others to change end results. Coaching leaders ask open-ended questions, push for alternative solutions to problems, and encourage reasonable risk-taking.[83]

Coaches Support and Encourage Others: As learning partners, coaches listen intently while being open to the perspectives of others. When employees vent, coaching leaders allow the venting without judgment, using encouragement as a tool to help them make progress toward their goals and recognize successes.[84]

---

[81] Ibid.
[82] Feldman, D.C. & Lankau, M.J. (2005). "Executive Coaching: A Review and Agenda for Future Research." *Journal of Management, 31*(6), 829-848
[83] Stoltzfus, T. (2005). *Leadership Coaching: The Disciplines, Skills, and Heart of a Christian Coach.* Virginia Beach, VA: Transformational Leadership Coaching.
[84] Ibid.

Coaches Drive Results: What is the outcome? Effective coaching leaders are intent on challenging others to achieve their goals. Coaching leaders help employees set meaningful goals and identify specific behaviors and steps for conquering them. Along the way, milestones and measures of success are used to encourage accountability.

Coaches Create a Culture of Coaching: They invest in and develop the right people to position them to coach and train others. This creates a pool of emergent coaches that leads to supporting a coaching mindset across the organization.

Organizations need Gen-X coaches to develop millennial leaders. Learning about the impact of coaches within a leadership setting will help organizations move in the right direction for future growth. As Millennials are future leaders, Gen-X coaches can develop ways to motivate them to build new skills and achieve goals. As this is achieved, Millennials will, in turn, be positioned to coach the next generation of leaders. These organizations will be on track to effectively develop quality leaders for the Kingdom of God as well as secular endeavors.

Questions to Consider:

1. *In your organization, how do Gen X'ers and Millennials partner to ensure the development of Millennial leadership?*
2. *Do you see coaching as a means to help Millennial leaders in your organization move forward with leadership styles that produce future growth?*
3. *How could coaching positively impact the leaders within your organization?*

CHAPTER 5:

LEADERSHIP COMPETENCIES

Leadership competencies such as communication, storytelling, and building a high-powered organizational design/culture are leadership skills that contribute to superior performance and leadership development. Using a competency-based approach to leadership helps organizations better identify and develop their next generation of leaders. Let's take a look at how the competencies of communication, storytelling, and building a high-powered organizational design/culture can create wins for organizations.

COMMUNICATION

Effective leadership communication is an essential leadership competency. It consists of those messages from a leader rooted in the values and culture of an organization. It is important for both Gen X'ers and Millennials to be powerful communicators in their organizations. Communicating a leadership message sometimes can be easy to deliver but not understood by many. Naturally, Gen X'ers and Millennials communicate differently. Effectively communicating leadership messages gives employees a better understanding of what a leader wants, what the organization needs, and how they fit into the picture for execution.

Types of Leadership Communicators: [85]

The Expert – Experts are the keeper of the mission, basing their communication and decision-making on facts and the relationship to the marketplace. They are skilled at transferring ideas, aligning expectations, inspiring action, and creating buy-in for vision.

The Visionary – Visionaries are leaders whose ardent belief in their cause outweighs their words, because their speaking style comes from deep within, from their inner core values. Their mission is to persuade and change points of view, with leadership continuing in their daily lives.

---
[85]Hackman, M.Z. & Johnson, C.E. (2013). *Leadership: A Communication Perspective*. Long Grove, IL: Waveland Press, Inc.

The Coach – The coach communicates by discovering what motivates people and leveraging that to help people succeed. Coaches are focused leaders who build teams, giving others the framework to apply their individual and collective talents.

The Transformer – Transformers are one-part visionary and one-part expert. They are on a mission to persuade and change their minds. They communicate where they are going and how to take people on the journey with them.

Communication is important because it increases morale, engagement, productivity, team collaboration, and cooperation. Effective communication helps to create better results for individuals, teams, and organizations. After reading the types of leadership communicators and their characteristics, which one resonates with you?

What Leadership Message Are You Sending?

Whether you are a Gen X'er or a Millennial, your leadership behavior and leadership message must be supported with effective communication in order to ensure buy-in and collaboration across the board. If you want your organization to reach new levels of achievement, you must master the art of clear communication.

Here Are the Four I's for Communicating Effectively:[86]

Inform – Leaders communicate with their people continually. Leaders need to be seen and heard frequently. They connect with their teams, create real influence, and build a culture of learning and collaboration.

Involve – Leaders are involved with all levels of their organization to solicit input. Leaders involve others to build a platform to raise issues and offer solutions. They seek to create meaning by making their message relevant to their

---
[86] Ibid.

team. Also, they listen to their team to gather information to make informed decisions. After all, discovery is the listening that sparks innovation.

Ignite – Leaders ignite people's imaginations about what they can do to make things better for themselves and their organizations. A leader's number one job is to inspire, motivate, and lead their team in the desired direction for the organization's success.

Invite – Leaders participate and invite others by creating messages that develop into win-win situations for the team. It is important to clearly articulate your vision and how your team will achieve the vision. This will help you find ways to infuse a sense of purpose on a continual basis for continued growth and productivity of your team.

To be a credible leader, you must also be trustworthy. Here is how credible leaders build trust:[87]

- Serve a purpose and serve those they lead.

- Live guiding principles and set consistent examples.

- Walk the talk and hold themselves accountable.

- Value feedback and ideas of others.

- Develop followers.

- Sustain hope within the organization.

---

[87] Economy, P. (2015). "7 Powerful Habits for Establishing Credibility as a Leader." Retrieved from https://www.inc.com/peter-economy/8-powerful-habits-to-establish-credibility-as-a-leader.html

If you follow these principles, you will avoid pitfalls in your leadership. When strong leadership messages are conveyed, leaders make it possible to build greater levels of trust, and as a result, more quality organizations.

STORYTELLING

Like effective communication, storytelling is a vital leadership competency that can significantly impact future leaders. More specifically, Gen-X leaders can indubitably help Millennials develop into valuable leaders by modeling great storytelling. This is a powerful vehicle to help this up-and-coming generation learn how to relate to the teams they lead, their organization, and specific tasks. Storytelling is an excellent way to help Millennials understand interpersonal skills such as how to work together, how to solicit and provide feedback, and which leadership and behavior approach is successful for various leadership scenarios. Gen X'ers can use deliberate stories to strategically convey values, experiences, and lessons to Millennials. Storytelling moves people to action! As a Gen-X ministerial leader, I have taught leadership seminars to Millennials in church settings. From leading and coaching Millennials, I learned to recognize the importance of embracing their differences and knowing intuitively how to connect the dots among those differences by the use of coaching conversations. For example, I have coached young Millennial women in business and church settings via my personal and professional stories. It was quite rewarding to use storytelling as a means to help teach natural and spiritual principles. As their conversation partner, it was from those transformative coaching conversations that those young women evolved out of dark places to accomplish their goals for impactful success in both their personal and professional lives.

As a church organization, storytelling is a beautiful picture of Proverbs 25:11, which reads, "A word fitly spoken is like apples of gold in a setting of silver." Likewise, Psalm 78:72 says, "With an upright heart, King David shepherded and guided with a skillful hand." Storytelling mirrors these scriptures because it helps leaders to be genuine, empathetic, helpful, and supportive of those they follow.

I have learned that storytelling is important in business and spiritual settings because it creates purposeful and captivating blueprints to inspire movement and change.

BUILDING A HIGH-POWERED ORGANIZATIONAL DESIGN/CULTURE

The third vital leadership competency is the ability to effectively impact organizational culture. For Millennial leadership development to be a success and the organization to be effective, the culture of the organization is key. Future leadership development ensures the design and culture of the organization function as the heartbeat and life-driving force to determine how things are done and how people behave in the organization. To achieve this, Millennials must be closely aligned to the culture for a healthy fit. Gen X'ers can help by "walking the talk," which means believing and exemplifying the vision and mission they rally everyone around.

To sum it all up, leadership communication is an essential leadership competency needed for organizations. It is important for Gen X'ers and Millennials to communicate well to help their organization operate effectively. Storytelling is also a vital leadership competency helping Gen-X leaders develop Millennials into valuable leaders by sharing stories that convey values, experiences, and lessons to Millennials. When communication and storytelling are present in organizations, they become high powered in their design and culture for Gen-X'ers and Millennials alike.

For Reflection:

Consider how the use of these three key leadership competencies could impact your effectiveness as a leader in reaching and impacting those you lead.

CHAPTER 6:

COACHING FOR MILLENNIAL LEADERSHIP DEVELOPMENT

Now that you have learned the value of leadership communication, storytelling, and becoming a high-powered organization for Gen X'ers and Millennials, let's consider how coaching for Millennial Leadership Development benefits organizations.

WHAT IS COACHING?

Coaching accelerates learning and shifts leaders from excellent performance to optimal performance. It is the process of equipping people with tools, knowledge, and opportunities needed for development and effectiveness.[88] Coaching is partnering with clients in a thought-provoking and creative process that inspires them to maximize their personal and professional potential.

Coaching Produces Transformative Change[89]

Via coaching, organizations will become an energized platform for questioning assumptions, stimulating reflection, creating or expanding options, and growing perspectives. Gen-X leaders will support Millennials by helping them tap into what really matters to them, offering encouragement and affirmation, facilitating access to resources along with the identification and removal of leadership barriers, creating systems of accountability, and celebrating small wins and managing setbacks.

COACHES ASK GREAT QUESTIONS

As coaches, Gen-X leaders will help Millennials analyze their character, their leadership style, and the culture of the organization. Those questions place value on strategy, personal initiative and responsibility, innovation, and continuous learning. For organizations, this paves the way for productivity and effectiveness and development of a deep bench of Millennial leaders with valuable skills and knowledge for succession plans for increased performance.

---

[88] Lewis, D.E. (2002, May 3). "Companies Are Hiring Coaches to Teach Executives How to Sharpen Management Skills and Communicate Effectively." Retrieved from www.bostonworks.com/globe/artciles/112600_coach.html.

[89] Lewis, D.E. (2002, May 3). Companies are hiring coaches to teach executives how to sharpen management skills and communicate effectively. Retrieved from www.bostonworks.com/globe/artciles/112600_coach.html.

COACHING AND SUCCESSION PLANNING

The common theme of leadership development and succession planning speaks to today's leaders in secular and ministerial organizations. Studies show 60.8 percent of organizations do not have formal succession plans.[90] This is an amazing statistic despite the overwhelming evidence that shows that developing a succession plan can help increase employee morale, reduce turnover, and increase the talent pool for promotable leaders within an organization, all of which can increase organizational effectiveness.[91]

Succession planning prepares for the future survival of the organization being a vehicle for both strategic planning and strategic foresight. An effective succession plan cultivates milestones in an organization, develops future strategic ideas, outlines strategic ventures, and defines the company's long and short-term goals. Without a succession plan contributing to the strength, growth, and success of an organization, catastrophes occur in the form of deterioration of productivity and effectiveness in the organization.[92]

APOSTLE PAUL AS A COACH

Paul's instructions, teaching, and leadership development established Timothy and Titus as future leaders to align with the organizational strategy to present Christianity with a clear mission, consistent core values, and leadership grounded in Christian faith.[93]

COACHING AND ASSESSMENTS FOR MILLENNIAL LEADERSHIP DEVELOPMENT

Apostle Paul identified Timothy and Titus as his key leaders to build churches and spread the gospel into different countries and cultures. Paul's assessment of their leadership was addressed with an extensive review of Timothy and Titus's characters and giftedness in their role

---

[90]Rothwell, W. J. (2010). *Effective Succession Planning: Ensuring Leadership Continuity and Building Talent From Within.* New York, NY: American Management Association.

[91]Ibid.

[92]Berendt, C. J., Christofi, A., Kasibhatla, K. M., Malindretos, J. & Maruffi, B. (2012). "Transformational Leadership: Lessons in Management for Today." *International Business Research,* 5(10), 227-232.

[93]Hollinger, T.D. (2013). "Leadership Development and Succession Planning: A Biblical Perspective for an Ethical Response." *Journal of Biblical Perspectives,* 5(1), 157-164.

of service.[94] Assessments and reviews (both formal and informal) yield clear-eyed, honest information about coachees, including their strengths and limitations as leaders and the challenges and opportunities that surround them.[95] With this information, the coach and coachee can discern where the opportunities for development are and where attention and energy can yield the greatest impact.

HOW CAN COACHING AND ASSESSMENTS HELP AN ORGANIZATION'S MILLENNIAL LEADERSHIP DEVELOPMENT?

A sound coaching plan, backed by assessments, cultivates and develops tomorrow's leaders, beginning with the alignment of leadership performance with strategy, along with an understanding of the type of leadership style(s) needed for successful leadership development.[96] The use of assessments creates the coaching interventions needed to deliver measurable results and build the next generation of leaders in business and ministry organizations for superior performance.[97]

THE VALUE OF ASSESSMENTS

There are thousands of assessments that will help your organization with Millennial leadership development. Assessments are valuable tools for ministerial and secular organizations to create purposeful dialogue and help leaders grow and serve professionally and spiritually. It is paramount to ensure the correct assessments are used to delve into meaningful and relevant coaching conversations for engagements and coaching plans. Such conversations will help your next generation of leaders clarify and organize their self-perceptions, recognize leadership and behavior patterns, and create actionable development goals. The marriage of coaching and assessments will help Millennials improve and develop in their personal and professional relationships for

---

[94]DeSilva, D. (2004). *An Introduction to the New Testament: Contexts, Methods & Ministry Formation*. Downers Grove, IL: InterVarsity Press.
[95]Van Velsor, E. McCauley C.D., Ruderman, (Eds). (2010). *The Center for Creative Leadership: Handbook of Leadership Development*. San Francisco, CA: John Wiley & Sons, Inc.
[96]Hansen, J. (2013). "Seven Steps for Effective Leadership Development." *Human Resources Magazine, 18*(5), 14-17.
[97]Trautmann, K., Maher, J. K. & Motley, D. G. (2007). "Learning Strategies as Predictors Of Transformational Leadership: The Case of Nonprofit Managers." *Leadership & Organization Development Journal, 28*(3), 269-287.

enhanced performance.

As a leader in finance and auditing, I have taken the Myers-Briggs MBTI, Strengths Finder, DISC, and a 360-degree feedback assessment on an annual basis to gauge leadership and feedback techniques. These assessments helped me discover my competencies, strengths, weaknesses, perception of myself, as well as the perceptions of others regarding my leadership. As a result, I developed an extensive understanding of how assessments work to bring out great leadership qualities and capacities. From my interactions with assessments, I also developed a love for coaching because it is the bridge to self-discovery and leadership development.

COACHING AND ASSESSMENTS REFLECTION

I had the awesome opportunity to coach a Millennial young lady in a church setting in 2018. She expressed to me that she was uncertain about her career aspirations. We embarked on setting up weekly coaching calls that sparked beneficial coaching conversations. From our confidential coaching conversations, we developed a coaching plan to explore career aspirations based on her assessment results. Additionally, I presented her with feedback, assessments, and weekly stretch assignments as actionable goals. I am pleased to say that after our coaching engagement, the young lady is flourishing in college, pursuing a Bachelor of Science in nursing, and has been recognized by her university with awards as an emergent leader.

Coaching and assessments are powerful tools to help Millennials take leaps and become more self-sufficient. When seasoned leaders utilize coaching and assessments, they partner with emergent Millennial leaders to unlock their potential to thrive within their ministerial or secular organization.

TAKEAWAY:

How can the use of assessments help your Gen-X leaders coach Millennials to emerge as powerful leaders?

CONCLUSION

Millennial leadership development is vital for organizations as they move into a rapidly changing future. Organizations must first know where they are going to have a great future, and then engage the workforce to carry it forward. In an era of constant innovation, it is important to understand that the future of work in any organization will involve Millennials. After all, this generation will represent nearly 75 percent of the workforce by 2025.

The BIG question is how will your organization or church look in the future? How will your leadership team look? Will Millennials be groomed for the future? You now have a blueprint of Millennial leadership development in relation to organizational leadership strategy, strategic foresight, and coaching as a panoramic view to birth strategies to create brilliant and innovative organizations that grow Millennial leaders.

Now is the time to pivot by encouraging your senior leaders to appreciate and envision the transformative impact Millennials can contribute to organizations. The future of your organization depends on empowering steps and solutions to develop a Millennial leadership development framework, thus helping leaders to implement an effective Millennial leadership development plan necessary for progression and transformational success.

www.ingramcontent.com/pod-product-compliance
Lightning Source LLC
Chambersburg PA
CBHW071228160426
43196CB00012B/2453